flinch & air

laura jane lee

Out-Spoken Press
London

Published by Out-Spoken Press,
Unit 39, Containerville
1 Emma Street
London, E2 9FP

A CIP record for this title is available from the British Library.

First edition published 2021
ISBN: 978-1-8384272-1-4

Typeset in Adobe Caslon
Design by Patricia Ferguson
Printed and bound by Print Resources

Out-Spoken Press is supported using public funding by the National
Lottery through Arts Council England and a grant from the Inclusive
Indies Fund administered by Spread the Word.

Supported using public funding by

**ARTS COUNCIL
ENGLAND**

to my tireless mother,
the strongest woman i know

Contents

Part I: 女也 ta

Part II: 我 ngo

Part III: mothering the land

Part I: 女也 ta

Tang Chu Ching 鄧珠清
(por-por 婆婆)

Tang was born in 1936, in a small farming village of Doumen District, Zhuhai in Guangdong Province, China. Born to a family of farmers, Tang was the third child and only girl in a family of four children. Tang had a relatively happy childhood, though poor, with a father who doted on her and was ahead of his time in recognizing daughters as equals to sons. They were largely unaffected by the Cultural Revolution as they were of the working class, but there were certain unfortunate events such as the accidental death of her sister at a very young age. At around 20, Tang left the village. She first faked illness and cited the pursuit of a cure in heading southwards, then, under the guise of marriage to a Stateside relative known only by a smart passport photo, made her way to Hong Kong, where she courted many suitors but settled on a sailor. Why she did, I cannot guess. From her I inherited mischief and vanity.
These are some of her stories.

my lover was a sailor boy

absence is the thing
that catches in the netting,

(when he would come back to me
smelling of brine and sea legs)

the thing
slippery and breathing,

(learning the sprawling vastness of the
heart, the one that is)

                                                 alive

undressed waiting

punctuating our
children

(clings to pining skeletons,
bathes the high days between rain)

blooming giddy every
season and again

                                                 yes

bold for love's
shivering,

(tossing
dry of the ocean's light,)

i resolve to the daily
wake, to high tide in empty

(bed, knowing my lover leans
in for a bent kiss on the cusp of)

land and
fluttering sea.

wee darling

wee darling,
that strangled night when the moth-black
rained with hushed
men-shouts, and high-strung the lightning
roughed our
little mud-hut,

you, wee
thing, how you slept whilst
creatures rang whinnying in the hollow-
weather, when mid-harvest our little boat
flipped like a fish-wish
in the storm-wash eve so
ma upped-and-went in the slurry
after pa, leaving us a flurry-bleed of
slum-thunder.

was just us, wee
one, you and me — you
snug as a bug to the moon-curve
of my small girl-spine
(ma left strapped you on white 'n' tight)
when all night round-and-round the
wet cement dark echoed like
our upside-down boat deep
in the belly of the lake; us
bottomed in the twilit-pour
diving for stretched-hours until
quietly your
morning-sleep seeped into mine
sister-body.

my wee babe,
your milk-breath sift
waning to my bone-shoulders, time yet
tarried skittish as lung-sacs in that
crack o' dawn, and when
thunder-panic last broke
with soft-sun i swear your
feathery child-soul too broke
flying through the glassless
window, like a chick-bird into the
still-dripping blue.

as if
strange, strange, strange the
thundershower milked you of all
rousing;

so
when ma came back,
she sat, howling,
and it rained some more.

爹 deh

i.

that yellow morning i was
delivered to your arms, you
pitied all the daughterless men.

the ones at the gambling house,
cigarette-stained, roughened, saying
daughters slender as rice stalks
are no use in the fields.

them paupers like you had mouths to feed,
crying, sucking,
screeching mouths
that had better not be a waste of good rice.
but after two sons,
that one yellow morning,
you pitied all the daughterless men as you
held my tiny creature body to the
hollow of your neck.

you had lost the wager,
at the gambling house
that yellow morning,
not a penny left —
so rocking me in my cloth swaddle
you gave me my name:
> *chu ching,*
> *clear pearl*
which in your heavy farmer's accent
sounded like
> *suu ching*
> *lost-it-all*

men with daughters have used up
all their bad luck! howled the
daughterless men at your gambling house.

bet they didn't know the cry of a daughter
as different from the cry of a son.
the cry of a daughter thaws and fills;
so it was instinctive that
come harvest,
full bushels of grain and gourds
and whatever you did not gamble away
were traded in the market next-town for
a pot of rouge and a jar of powder
so a child might giggle to her
painted girlish face in the
one cracked
mirror of a
bare-bones house.
you even insisted that i have shoes —
(many girls didn't) —
so i could join the Republicans' scouts
which later
became the Communists' marching band.

but alas, even then
with a daughter a
poor man is
poor.

so when instead of
marrying a farmer who promised
fifty cows
your daughter decided to leave
the village for Britain's shining
crown colony;

you went down
(that one yellow morning)
to the gambling house
and won fifty cows' worth of money
from all the daughterless men you pitied.

ii.

i won fifty cows' worth of money
from the men at the gambling house
that one yellow morning
you decided to leave this slow
place for Hong Kong,
eschewing marriage to the
man who promised
fifty cows to
this poor farmer.

i remember
how the Communists' marching band
used to be the
Republicans' scouts;
how i insisted you have shoes
so you could join —
(many girls couldn't) —
and how my child you
sat in our bare-bones house with the
one cracked
mirror
giggling to your girlish face,
painted with the rouge and powder
i bartered for in the market next-town
with that harvest's
bushels,
grains, gourds and

whatever i hadn't gambled away.

it's instinctive:
the cry of a daughter
is different
from the cry of a son.
it thaws, fills, they didn't have
the pleasure of knowing that, i bet,
all them daughterless men
at my gambling house, howling
men with daughters have used up
all their bad luck!

     clear pearl,
     chu ching—
your mother said it sounded like
when i told her i had
     lost-it-all,
     suu ching
all my money's
worth at the gambling house
gone that yellow morning i
rocked you in your cloth swaddle,
but as i held the world in
your tiny creature body to the
hollow of my neck,
i pitied all the daughterless men.

paupers, they too had
mouths to feed,
crying, sucking,
screeching mouths;
and two sons later i can tell you that
daughters are not a
waste of good rice and

no,
i could not bear to have you,
frail as a rice stalk,
work a day in the field.

so when you were swaddled, your
call newly alive,
i counted the fresh days and yellow mornings,
the men with their sons,
and considered the way i was
delivered to you
as a man with
such fortune.

tears

there are some times
i remember to
look at your face and am
reminded of
scissors.

your face in the dust-dance
film house
that
ash-shroud of sorrow
eyes sunken into wells
marred by feature-length Cantonese tragedy.

可憐。天下。父母。心
over and over, the same perforation:
woeful are the hearts of all
fathers & mothers
beneath the heavens.

and tears come as a flurry of knives
and tears come as a flurry of knives.

Yang Chang Man 卓春梅

Yang was born in 1944 to a Malaysian Chinese family, in a sleepy village in Malaysia. Yang's family eventually moved to Singapore, where she was formally educated in Chinese schools, and went on to study Biology, Fisheries and Copepods. She worked in Zoology and Marine Biology, before a turn in fortune (which direction, who could say?) saw her appointed Curator at the Department of Zoology, which would soon take over the Raffles Collection. With her scientific training as a marine biologist, she took on the mammoth task of caring for the 130,000 specimens as they were shuffled from one temporary home to the next before the opening of Lee Kong Chian Natural History Museum in 2015. It was a thankless job and she was armed only by her wits in the fight against the tide of time, humidity and men. Some say she is the wife of Noah; others, mother of the Animals.
I know her as a woman with a name.

noah's wife

after
the men
had sought out
two of every animal
herded them, male and female
on board that insurmountable eyesore —
she found herself, at once, put to
work, conferred stewardship
of exotic beasts, guardian
of a vast menagerie of
creatures, skittish
in their skins,
bones
restless as
children lay stacked
in coffin-crates, cramped,
refuge from all the rain where
under the zinc roofs she tended on them,
kept them cool, dry, pestless with poison,
which soon ravaged her blood.
a tireless wench adrift
with the fishes in
her own sea of
formalin
whilst the men
were off doing things
of UTMOST IMPORTANCE —
running the ark, keeping them
afloat, the animals forgotten all
one hundred and thirty thousand of them
tacked up squalid, spooled in red tape
midst the deluge where at night she

lies awake, telegraphs God
WHY/ HOW & WHEN the
waters will ever recede?
yet despite her best,
some wild things
begin to rot, the
smell of sick
carcass on
her hair,
it was
grit
that kept
her going for
sixteen years, plucky
as the backbone of a whale, as
more than once the men contemplate
slinging them overboard,
the women to follow.
angered, she wires
God another:
REPRIEVE.
looks
within
herself for the
matriarchal insistence,
to keep every critter and brute
on board, preserved for the children
of her children and the unborn to come.

                                    in time,
                          the seafarers dock
                      on a mountain far from
                where they boarded and Noah

emerges onto dry ground, declaring
himself God's loyal Servant, his men
Faithful Keepers of the Animals.
this is when she
wistfully yields
her load
to the
land

it will be years before we learn her name

Lee Mei 李美

Chuang Tzu and Hui Tzu were strolling along the dam of the Hao River when Chuang Tzu said, 'See how the minnows come out and dart around where they please! That's what fish really enjoy!'

Hui Tzu said, 'You're not a fish—how do you know what fish enjoy?'

Chuang Tzu said, 'You're not I, so how do you know I don't know what fish enjoy?'

Hui Tzu said, 'I'm not you, so I certainly don't know what you know. On the other hand, you're certainly not a fish—so that still proves you don't know what fish enjoy!'

Chuang Tzu said, 'Let's go back to your original question, please. You asked me how I know what fish enjoy—so you already knew I knew it when you asked the question. I know it by standing here beside the Hao.' [1]

[1] *The Complete Works of Chuang Tzu*, translated by Burton Watson (Columbia University Press, 1968)

fish wishes from a 2-chambered heart

1. to make no choices
2. to heed the matchmaker's order
3. to be brokered something you can swallow
   (see: a coin, or affection)
4. to be tender, and fresh
5. to carry my own flesh to the sea
6. to swim these careless bones
7. to hold a mouthful of plastic questions
8. to consider cardiac anatomy foolish
9. to roam seven seas with five fins
   (last seen: pacific)
   (missing: dorsal fin)
10. to be unbound from the island
11. to cut through this hill
    (see: Mount Davis)
12. to be coated with optimism
13. to escape marination
    (ceviche: bitter, sour, spice)
14. to roll up the gate every morning
15. to not know that time is a thief
    (stolen: light, shadow)
16. to have the long years throw themselves

17. to finally allow myself to sleep
    (on: his bed)
    (see: beside him)
18. to lose count of the days
19. to be restless under my skin
20. to keep me my scales
21. to talk about the weather
    (that: which i have weathered)
22. to sit by the window
23. to let him hold me
    (under: storm and sun)
24. to wish as a fish can
    (see: in a net)

知魚
李冠麟

不必抉擇 媒妁一聲確立 愛他
心的困惑 游在山海兩峽 隨波吧

我無懼嗎 情願嗎 唇邊有話
似魚又怕 往江海出嫁 去吧

魚在渴望魚在喝 一生浪蕩
登島背鰭割 摩星嶺踏過崗

即使豁達 嘗盡腥苦與辣 對嗎
拉起鐵閘 誰料光陰有賊 人生吧

我挨餓嗎 難受嗎 鄉情總念掛
看魚在那 大海等出價 算吧

魚在渴望魚在喝 一生浪蕩
登島背鰭割 摩星嶺踏過崗
明白際遇成定案 充斥碰撞
生於這魚網 堅守寸地尺方

鱗未脫落仍硬朗 久經跌蕩
當他抱著我 西區驟然已滄桑
陪著我如常渡過 驚風駭浪
即使欠晴朗 家室裏或有光

ma 媽

the heart of the matter

is perhaps knowing
that i must survive
you
all these years existing again and
again, your tongue a
half-step into the void wanting for
answers knowing that i must hurt
you
that shivering joy
that singing ache in the
cavity you call a
womb
now where your heart sleeps
every night wringing itself
out every
night when you
ask a daughter
'what's the matter?'
knowing that i must write
you
one of these
many
days

michelle

michelle

a ceramic loss

the country is always losing
itself in my bed/ i do not understand
but this is a museum denoting
the coldness of silver in which drowns itself a people

>   how my kin found their
>   toes in strange gravel to buy
>   clock faces and i all lost with my
>   sweated irons far up in the greens those
>   years there was no need at
>   all for repatriation

in my bed now that
i have gotten around to reaching into
the exhibit a *BONE CHINA BLUE* breath
to my touch feeling so carelessly curated
a life this/ no longer
dreaming of losing the salvage

>   he walks out of my room and
>   always from me his face to the sky/ not
>   lost/ just away just thinking what to do to
>   the beginning of/ so painting my face on/
>   this loss/ this woman is always losing no
>   longer/ nor sleeps itself in your head

hebe

grieving in both directions

often one goes hunting for grace
rifled, as one does when heavied/ so
to go stalking this kindness
thick with being irrevocable/
pregnant with forgiveness you
realise/ that this is the wrong crib for a
mother's translation of daughterhood of
grieving in both directions/ heaving all
bodies of grace in believing that solace
what hurriedly passes and passes —

often
one goes killing for healing

gei

this side of the border

and picture this: a wisp of a girl
born   this side of the border
to another life   entirely
different   by fate
from birth   to leave
from home   to strange city
that side of the border   at twelve she crosses
over to our   oceans
murky fisheries   to fish for the
wishes of   dining tables
men waiting   to catch
her girlhood   in a net like
threatened   dreams

child drifting   in the sea
into womanhood   on a small sampan
alone   in cold dusk
imagine   how cold
she must have been   not even fourteen
(how terrified)   she manages to
leave the water for   land
a factory   a job in Bangkok.

fifteen   in thick city
choking on   toxic fumes of
cheap paints   gold spray
jewellery factory   never stop
just gives more work to   nimble tireless fingers
her   making
for the vanity of   girls her age
an industry   working girls to bone.

28

her luck takes a turn for the better
domestic work life
tending to a retired couple
comfortably upper-middle class they take her on.
between cooking and cleaning between folding, washing
her small soft body finds there is no time to dream
no space to grow stranded far from home
only just where she started she lays her heart to rest

this side of the border a girl her age for whom
she serves dinner work is not an option.
she sends her meagre wage back to her family
in Burma, where dreams are
three meals of whatever she wants them to be,
rice as long as it
is the result of her hard work is an honourable pursuit.

they enroll her in literacy classes
Thai and English do not teach her to dream.
perhaps if she were younger
school could have planted the seeds of ambition
the desire for more could have taken root.

but here and now
in this story she is happy with
what she has the rice
is enough for her and she wants nothing but
the promise to never fish again.
of tomorrow she is hopeful
holds the chance to wear
all that she knows her only want:
she will one day have that gold-painted bracelet,
of dreams. her own.

29

june

yet to be

// those years we too were flies in syrup
plastered face-up face-down glowing like
the rain or else the pavement under
which we brace in conch shells, our
bones silent under skins ever so hungry
for contact for crying out loud and kissing
lovers dying lovers burning all around the
air is thinning to a halt in the looking glass
and i would explain in not so many words
as you prepared to break again as we
were Not Yet Titled we were not even
close but that night you'd bend and again
and bend and again and i'd take a cue
from the real world and internalize my
externalities then know we both were
miles away from being the sun those boys
with soft lips and eyes searing all those
years when we too were flies in syrup
digging our insides clean and i'd hurt for
your faults and not my sins and know
nothing we could say to each other would
make any sound but at least we lived my
love at least we survived //

Part II: 我 ngo

the summer critter speaks not of frost
夏蟲不可語冰
A BEAUTIFUL MIND

do not trespass with perhaps/ do not
ponder why the brief critter sheds its days
like that/ that summer is more of a
reprieve than trapping home/ that it will
try and try and not find the word for frost/
that it does not know at all that the world
can stay colder than fire/ which is torrid/
that you can even drown in the
intolerable light/ in its dreams white is a
figment/ & melting is but a tributary of
perishable air/ i will be lost/ i will be
impossible/ spent like an envelope singing
my eyes shut/ always forgetting/ always/
this duet a starved type of blue

all flesh

the next time this happens you
will sit in the fire
and listen
to the quiet tax of your existence.

you and every world,
at once leaning
giant into this mouthless
grief —
swimming in all that

mangled joy;
your singing ache
crooning like a mutilated canary:
all flesh is terrible

and terrible you are,
in the fire
piecemeal and faceless but always
planning for some naked elation.

i too do not know how you do this:

you survive it

your heart blooming
like an ambulance.

the days of the dog

(pastiche of 'The Year of the Kiss' by Reid Mitchell, for drg)

those were the days that the dog was in
charge, Cerberus all, and there were
always dogs in charge, added snow after
snow to perennial night, with no
smothering until heavy, so that the days
never ended, so i always woke up the
same time tomorrow, as there were
soundtracks yet to die to, until February
till April became the dizziest on record,
and the highest purge rate the body had
borne since the day you went stir crazy.
and still, you got cabin fever with poor
sunlight, and you tried to pry open your
unplugged mouth to get the last bits of
food out, and still thought you would be
in love with him always, and that he
deserved not only to be forgiven but to be
cherished tenderly and let walk all
over you.

those were the climes in which bathroom
tiles were heated, cried on, and scrubbed
with raw hands, so that you could go to
sleep in peace in your blue coffin-bed;
sitting by the laboratory window
watching it rain, grey onto the water, the
spot you decided that biologically
speaking, if you stopped eating, all of you
would *become* hunger, and there would
be no ghosts so you may for sanity's sake
lock yourself in a library, sleep on

scratchy hall seats unfolded with fingers,
emptying yourself completely in a
warm-lit bathroom stall, as salty and
bloody as love, as grief, for those were the
days your heart had no choice but to stop,
those were the days of the dog —
which days could never be worse than,
and will always be.

tomorrow, and, and

tomorrow knows   nothing   of how you
stood   wavering   and tomorrow
at the slightest   precipice
and   tomorrow   slinking songward
rhythm   day unto   day knowing
chronology   has   to be put in   its
place   just as the heart   travels   miles
per hour   unreported   till last syllable
of last night   shewn lives   hurrying
to no parole   with promise   of
symmetrical dust   dancing on   cremation
never snuffed   never nothing   fire
throwing shadows   stepping shadows
waltzing eye   true as   life playing
game   execution   impeccable
through even   faltering   the hour of day
uncertain   and will   re-echo always your
standing at the edge   a tale you
marred with grace   full fanfare and dread
touching   almost   everything

flinch & air

woke up wanting to kiss you/ in
teeth-brushing and fingernail/ in batwing
and sleep/ under wanting to drink you/
beneath flinch and air/ between
hypnotism and spake/ i am/ between
language and i am/ amphibious/ within
thick and pocket/ but your spend and
your disappoint/ to exist and that thereof/
what if i/ just want to complicate you?/
with radio/ with mouth/ for best or for
worst/ mine/ to tonic and to lip/ what to
have/ and what/ to hold

force majeure

the outside storming seethes through, no gritting
teeth can keep out the most perfect headache anymore
panic carefully,
see that the mulch too cries: *assume candescence* —
invert all this rain! realise
how expensive this ornament of a sound
this tall order simmering like a
tongue, vacuum
freeze-dry this damp restlessness
and this thrashing like air
even this
lurching straight into you tastes insidious
such a lovely,
lovely
trouble — being under you
and this thunder feeling?
tonight you shall find
your own self downside-up logic
will do the trick and none of it
will survive so try
me i must i promise to
sliver you like
a heart

drawn downward

at some point you might
decide to love me at all and
find it entirely incorrigible to even
backtrack upwards into the spectrum of visible light, most
will recommend that for safety at a bullet's stretch you must
follow the signage of the breadcrumb trails they
do not last quite long enough for sustenance but they never lie so
you might as well assume my intentions
being solid enough to rap your knuckles on and that
the sky being right side down, my hollows
will float like an antithesis to
what i am really made of, this terrible texture that
will float like an antithesis to
the sky being right side down, my hollows
being solid enough to rap your knuckles on and that
you might as well assume my intentions
do not last quite long enough for sustenance but they never lie so
follow the signage of the breadcrumb trails they
will recommend for safety at a bullet's stretch you must
backtrack upwards into the spectrum of visible light, most
find it entirely incorrigible to even
decide to love me at all and
at some point you might

Part III:
mothering the land

Sweet Like a Bao

Michael Ondaatje's poem, 'Sweet Like a Crow')

Is like the red of a lampshade

t

pping of fish on the chopping block
like swearing taxi drivers
like a leaky AC unit, like the innards of a
too-hot dimsum, like a stray cat meowing,
a chow-mein being chowed
a truck mixing concrete
a canton opera at the Central Pier.
Like an Octopus card beep,
like a plethora of neon light boxes
like pergolas in the park,
a chestnut shell, an MTR crowd
when the doors are closing
like the speed meter on a red minibus
like Char Siu Bao,
an old-style cash register, like a million
Mark Six balls being scrambled, like someone
trying to sub-divide a flat,
the opening jingle of a TV documentary three doors down,
a really uninteresting PSA on Radio One,
the sound of a waiter when someone is slow to order,
like durians being opened on a rock
like a whole housing estate airing out their dirty laundry
on a Monday, like an enthusiastic beginner
shuffling the Mahjong tiles, like Cha Chaan Teng,
like 7 oranges rolling down the slope
like 5 pickpockets pickpocketing
like the sound I heard when having an afternoon sleep
and someone tried to tune the piano.

In Extradition
after Chris van Wyk

She was shot in the eye with a bearing ball
She framed herself
She ruptured her eye while rioting
She framed herself
She ruptured her eye while rioting
She was shot in the eye with a bearing ball
She framed herself while rioting
She ruptured a bearing ball
She framed a bearing ball
She framed herself in the eye with a bearing ball while rioting
She was shot in the eye by rioters while rupturing
She framed herself with a bearing ball
She rioted with a bearing ball while rupturing
She framed a rupturing while rioting.

muscovado (nov 12, 2019; cuhk)
黑 ■

[retelling of a story from a medical student at The Chinese University]

now i have learnt that
it was always
something watching us with
the parlance of sugar

the most edible lie is how
starved you are for acridity —
how eyes flickered when you
said the people started
putting it on their tongues, sick as
syrup

i will always remember it as a
disembarkment of molasses.
effigy of grime come to cling,
smell of armed men.
how the air tasted haphazard before
you started trespassing from the
clogged highway,
rounds, canisters.

all across the land
you and i were watched on LCD.
water found its way in through any of
the thickjammed exits.

an unfamiliar quench began pooling
the dormitories.

even now i think of how young
their bodies were, positively juvenile

when the siege
began and how,
by the time the older ones repatriated
they were already in the sweetthick mire.

by second dusk
you brought in your big toys
billeted them on our bridge,
chock full of your lewd blue.

how do you not understand, even now,
that no one
at all likes building barricades?

imagine the fear of a tomorrow so terrible
that eggs shell themselves for oblation on
highwalls.

yesterday i was thinking of how
despite all their professorship,
they could not stop
all the young limbs being shot blue
from now i will see many up close
tend likewise to bloodied gapes but none
with such saccharine colour.

after some tomorrows
the streams here have spattered.
rolling off, as they do,
to quell the arsoned city.
and i
am only just realizing how many half-
lives have been taken, why
a city in vertigo
thinks hyperglycemia is the
sweetest way to die.

Acknowledgements

An earlier version of '爹 deh' was previously published in the *Mekong Review*.

'fish wishes from a 2-chambered heart' was published in *Metaphor as Metamorphosis: A Journal*. It was inspired by the Cantonese song 知魚, with lyrics by Kenelm Lee.

An earlier version of 'a ceramic loss' was published in *Bath Magg*.

'the summer critter speaks not of frost 夏蟲不可語冰' was awarded the Sir Roger Newdigate Prize and is published in *Napkin Poetry Review*.

'In Extradition' was previously published in *HK01*.

'Sweet Like a Bao' was previously published in the *Proverse Poetry Prize 2018 Anthology*.

Thanks must be given to my alpha and beta readers, in particular Joshua Ip, D Mortimer, April Yee, Sean Wai-Keung, Samantha Yau, Natalie Linh Bolderston and Jonathan Chan,

my tutor Jack Underwood and the Foundation Workshop in Creative Writing at Goldsmiths University for workshopping some of these poems,

Crispin Rodrigues and the Publishing Support Group for their feedback,

Ben, for reading (suffering) the first draft of every single poem,

and Joelle, for making this possible at all.

Other titles by Out-Spoken Press

Email: press@outspokenldn.com